Homeward

Layla Ali Sultan

ISBN   978 - 2 - 8399 - 3444 - 2

I heard you

I tried to run away
I tried to drift away
I tried to fly away

Forgetting myself
Forgetting the world
Forgetting You

I closed my eyes
I stuffed my ears
I turned off my mind

In the midst of my very own chaos
You still came to find me

In the midst of my very own fantasy
You still came to find me

In the midst of my very own fire
You still came to find me

You drifted in
through the images

You drifted in
through the stories

You drifted in
through the songs

I heard You
I felt You
I held You

How could I have doubted You?
How could I have blamed You?
How could I have pushed You away?

When You were the One carrying me
When You were the One cradling me
When You were the One catching me

Even when I turned my face away
Even when I burned my faith away
Even when I bolted away

You were the One guiding me
You were the One saving me
You were the One loving me

When I hit the wall
When I hit the water
When I hit my head

I called You
I asked You
I begged You

But didn't want to hear Your answer
But didn't want to understand Your answer
But didn't want to see Your answer

I ran into the marshes
I ran through the crags
I ran to the summit

Bleeding
Burning
Bending

Breaking
Crying
Praying

But all the while

I was pretending to be like them
I was pretending to live like them
I was pretending to think like them

You knew it was all a lie

At night,

I could hear my heart reminding me of the truth
I could hear my soul reminding me of the truth
I could hear my lies reminding me of the truth

But still,

I kept on burying myself
I kept on drowning myself
I kept on numbing myself

Little by little

I dragged myself out of the ravine
I dragged myself towards the forest
I dragged myself to the river

As I swam
I healed

As I fought the current
I healed

As I braved the weather
I healed

I came back
I came back Home
I came back to You

Wake up to the Truth

It was the perfect match
It was the perfect man
It was the perfect story

But it wasn't real
But it's wasn't you
But it wasn't me

It was a spell
It was a hex
It was a curse

I woke up in the middle of the night

The cold wind was twisting the trees
The harsh wind was twirling the chimes
The freezing wind was tweaking

It was so cold
It was so lonely
It was so drab

The horrendous wind was making the trees weep
The monstrous wind was howling through the trees
The murderous wind was freezing the birds as they slept

There was no music
There were no colors
There was no one

I could only hear the moans
I could only hear the battering
I could only hear the bells

Darkness was hovering
Pain was hovering
Despair was hovering

Oh how I wish I could go back!

Even if it was madness
Even if it was delusional
Even if it was a chimera

Give it back to me

The golden glory
The gentle wings
The luminous embrace

I beg tee

This tempest is terrible
This howling is terrible
This loneliness is terrible

I am left with my doubts
I am left with my fears
I am left with myself

I try to close my eyes
I try to hum a song
I try to feel it again

but it's lost

Because I know

It was just a dream
It was just an illusion
It was just a mirage

I cannot escape this torment
I cannot escape this cold
I cannot escape this bitterness

And there comes a mossy fairy
And there comes a misshapen shadow
And there comes an otherworldly creature

Bestowing a mighty gift to me
Bestowing a murky phial to me
Bestowing a silver web to me

I am the daughter of the tempestuous wind
I am the mother of the deadly frost
I am the the granter of your utmost wish

You have called in despair
You have cursed in vain
You have given me pearls of salt

Here, here child
Do not cry

Here, here child,
Tell me everything

Here, here child,
It will all soon be over

What do you desire?
What do you miss?
What do you beg for?

I will take you away from this place
I will whisk you out of this storm
I will pull you away from this abyss

But her eyes have the silver glint of a sword
But her smile has the red shadow of a wound
But her fingers have the ashen tint of the grave

She shakes her little phial and let me see all that I
could have

I see his smiling face
I see my smiling face
I see our smiling lives

It seems so surreal
It seems so beautiful
it seems so perfect

Too perfect

Like the delicate lace of the black widow
Like the gentle twinkle of the supernova
Like the perfumed petals of the Hyacinth

No.

I don't seek deceitful perfection
I don't seek empty beauty
I don't seek unreal happiness

I want the truth

Let it bight
Let it freeze
Let it slap

Go away

And as I looked

She crumpled to the floor into a

puddle of decay
puddle of putrefaction
puddle of worm eaten dirt

I open my door

I let the wind knot my hair
I let the wind freeze my tears
I let the wind torn away the pages

Let it go
Let it fly
Let it break

I embrace you

Darkness
Loneliness
Cold

You are my companions now

Your moans
Your screeches
Your whispers

are my music

Let me sink into slumber
Let me sink into dreamlessness
Let me sink into nothingness

To awaken tomorrow

as the pink dawn is stretching
as the warm sun is shining
as vain hope is rising

Let me wake up again
when it's all forgotten

Let me wake up again
when all the trees are all bent

Let me wake up again
when the leaves are all scattered

Let me rise again
when a new world is waking

Let me rise again
when a new world is building

Let me rise again
when a new world is healing

all the woes
all the curses
all the wounds

And that God's grace

and that God's face
And that God's peace

is embracing us
is protecting us
is gathering us

in a womb of light
in a womb of love
in a womb of truth

Like a child

My Love,
My Heart,
My All,

Have I deceived You?
Have I forgotten You?
Have I lost You?

I was so angry
I was so sad
I was so bitter

Like a child

who had lost her favorite toy
who had been refused a treat
who had lost his mother

I've been wandering aimlessly
I've been burning and grieving
I've been smothering my inner light

Punishing myself

By depriving myself from my Solace
By depriving myself from my Absolution
By depriving myself from my Home.

Forgive me
Shelter me

Wait for me

Even when I turned myself away from You
Even when I blamed You in silence
Even when I ignored You

You didn't leave me
You didn't forget me
You didn't lead me astray

You kept on shining on me
You kept on steering me
You kept on cradling me

Until I woke up
Until I grew up
Until I stood up

To bow
To prostrate
To melt

Into Your warm embrace
Into Your boundless embrace
Into Your soothing embrace

Oh dearest Love
Oh dearest Heart
Oh dearest God

Forgive me

For tarnishing this light
For tarnishing this life
For tarnishing this body

It is all Yours

And You are My Home
And You are my Creator
And You are My Destination

How can express

This gratitude
This thankfulness
This blessedness

I was seeking
I was begging
I was crying

You are the One I was looking for
You are the One I was longing for
You are the One I was dying for

Nothing
No place
No one

Can fill this little box
Can fill this endless universe
Can fill this human heart

Only You
Only You
Only You

You are the Knower of all things

Oh You know
how I cherish this dream

Oh you Know
how I pray for this dream

Oh you know
how I long for this dream

You are the keeper of my dreams
You are the keeper of my prayers
You are my keeper.

And the truth is

it's worth nothing
it's worth dust
It's worth dirt

If it's driving me away from

Your Love
Your Arms
Your Will.

I thought he was my way towards you
I thought he was my gift bestowed by you
I thought he was what you wanted for me

but I must have
taken my desires for Yours

but I must have
taken my foolish dreams for Your design

but I must have
taken my wishes for Your command

Forgive me

For my blindness
For my foolishness
For my silliness

I fell in the trap
I fell in the well
I fell in the pit

As easily as a curious kitten
As easily as a new born
As easily as a foolhardy bird

My wings are trapped in this mess
My wings are broken in this hell
My wings are flightless in this nightmare

Oh dear Lord!

How wrong I was!
How foolish I was!
How childish I was!

But the worst is

This blindness
This darkness
This confusion

What is the truth?
What is reality?
What is Your will?

I'm so tired
I'm so broken
I'm so lost

I thought I had found another path
I thought I had found another anchor
I thought I had found another haven

Am I wrong?

Should I turn around?
Should I leave?
Should I run away?

Or should I still believe in the best
Or should I still believe in my hope
Or should I still believe in my prayers

The path of righteousness

Is filled with light
is filled with hope
is filled with love

And still my heart believes that

I should still hope
I should still be steadfast

I should still pray

But is it Your command?
Or only wishful thinking?

But is it Your will?
Or is it only my will?

But is it Your voice
Or is it only my twisted dreams?

Please tell me
Please set me free
Please save me

Take it all from me
the love and the pain

Take it all from me
the hopes and the despairs

Take it all from me
the dreams and the doubts

Who am I to demand?
Who am I to desire?
Who am I to command?

My life is Yours
My heart is Yours
My soul is Yours

I belong to you

Give me strength
Give me wisdom

Give me patience

Should I wait or fight?

Should I leave or stay?

Should I stand up or kneel?

Is it time to let go?
leave it all to You

Is it time to let go?
bestow it all to You

is it time to let go?
entrust it all to You

But before I do it
and trust You

How far should I go?
How much should I do?
How much should I give?

Tell me
because I have no idea

How arrogant of me
to think I knew it all

You are the Knower of all things
You are the Keeper of all secrets
You are the Cherisher of all hearts

Dearest Love,

Show me the way
Show me the truth
Show me my strength

So that I may best serve You,

20

To give - For you

I cannot be
What they want me to be

I cannot do
What they want me to do

I cannot give them
What they want me to give

It's my fault
I love too much

It's my fault
I care too much

It's my fault
I give too much

And they keep hoping
And they keep expecting
And they keep asking

I give
I love
I share

All that I can

But not anymore
But not tonight
But not again

I am too tired
I am too drained
I am too wasted

I thought I could be like You
I thought I could love like You
I thought I could give like You

But I am not You
But I am far from being You
But I am not God

As much as I want
my strength has a limit

As much as I want
my love has a limit

As much as I want
my compassion has a limit

I wish I could give it all
I wish I could outshine the sun
I wish I could love them all

But I am so worn out
But I am so weak
But I am so empty

The more you give
the more you get

The more you love
the more love you get

The more you share
the more you have in return

It sounds so poetic
It sounds so beautiful
It sounds so true

Maybe there's something wrong
Maybe I'm doing it wrong
Maybe I'm wrong…

In the sea
In the forest
In the mountains

There's harmony
There's equilibrium
There's serenity

In every sunbeam
In every moonbeam
In every raindrop

Oh dear God,

You told us
You asked us
You commanded us

To be just
To be constant
To be level headed

But I wished so much
But I prayed so much
But I believed so much

That I should be full of light
That I should be full of love
That I should be full of care

That I should love them all
That I should help them all
That I should save them all

But I am a mere individual
But I am a mere human
But I am a mere girl

So take them my Lord
So embrace them my Lord
So love them my Lord

I was wrong to think

That it was my duty
That it was my destiny
That it was my imperative

To give

All my love
All my being
All my soul

But they are your children
But they are your creatures
But they are yours.

Like me

I am no saint
I am no savior
I am no priestess

I am your child
I am your creature
I am yours

I wasn't born to save him
I wasn't born to save them
I wasn't born to save the world

I was born to love You
I was born to serve You
I was born to obey You

You are our Deity
You are our Savior
You are our Guide

You are our Love
You are our Light
You are our Hope

You are our Eternity
You are our Present
You are our Forever

You are my Protector
You are my Parent
You are my Peace

To you I bestow

my dreams
my trust
my endeavors

To you I bestow

Those I love
Those I help
Those I hate

To you I bestow

my inner light
my inner love
my inner pain

How foolish I was
How arrogant I was
How self destructing I was

I am nothing

Without Your grace
Without Your love
Without Your care

To you I bestow

my crushed dreams
my crushed hopes
my crushed compassion

I cannot do it anymore
I cannot love anymore
I cannot care anymore

There isn't anything left in me
There isn't any light left in me
There isn't any spark left in me

I'm wounded
I'm barren
I'm consumed

They want more
They ask for more
They expect more

Is it true?
Is it my imagination?
Is it my nightmare?

I gave all my love
I gave all my compassion
I gave all my faith

I can't want anything from them
I can't ask anything from them
I can't expect anything from them

You are the only one I beg
You are the only one I ask
You are the only one I expect from

You are the only one I really need
You are the only one I really want
You are the only one I really desire

The rest is illusion
The rest is idleness
The rest is vain

As long as You forgive me
As long as You protect me
As long as You love me

I can go on
I can go farther
I can go towards You

Show me how much you love me
Show me how far I should go
Show me how I should serve you

Don't leave me here with them
Don't leave me here in the darkness
Don't leave me here in nothingness

Embrace me
Encompass me
Enfold me

Take my dreams
Take my failings
Take my victories

Take everything

Love them

Oh how they fall
one by one

Oh how they leave
one by one

Oh how they deaden themselves
one by one

Their smiles freeze
Their eyes darken
Their embraces stiffen

Where is their heart?
Where is their soul?
Where is their love?

My heart bleeds
My heart cries
My heart breaks

For what they were
For what they are
For what they will be

Now that they have taken this path
Now that they have closed their heart
Now that they have broken their spirit

Wandering listlessly

Roaming aimlessly
Dying in vain

But they don't want my tears
But they don't want my sorrow
But they don't want my love

They think they know it all
They think I don't know anything;
But You know it all

Oh my Lord
Forgive them

Oh my Lord
Love them

Oh my Lord
Guide them

As you have forgiven me
As you have loved me
As you have guided me

Don't let them give up on you
Don't give up on them
Is there any hope left?

This is my hope
This is my wish
This is my prayer

That they see Your Light
That they see Your Truth
That they see Your Love

I am Yours

I just want to scream
I just want to yell
I just want to holler

To rip it all off
To burn it all
To destroy it all

I hate those feelings
I hate myself
I hate you

I hate being trapped like this
I hate being trapped in myself
I hate being trapped because of you

I want to be strong
I want to be a hero
I want to be a warrior

I want to be victorious
I want to be honorable
I want to be a rockstar

I want to scream
I want to yell
I want to holler

I want to kick
I want to punch

I want to push

Push it all away
Push these dark clouds away
Push you away

I want to forget my words
I want to forget your silence
I want to forget reality

I despise reality
I despise myself
I despise weakness

I want glory
I want victory
I want freedom

I am so damn tired
I am so damn lost
I am so damn disgusted

I tried
I believed
I hoped

I stopped sleeping
I stopped living
I stopped doubting

And I had to face this

wall of silence
ocean of silence
abyss of silence

No words
No feelings
No smile

Are you scared?
Are you mad?
Are you bored?

Do you even care?
Do you even care about this?
Do you even care about me?

Am I in all this alone?
Am I living it all in my head?
Am I imagining all this?

I called on You God
I prayed to You God
I begged You God

And there's your answer
And there's your sign
And there's your miracle

But I still don't understand it
But I still don't grasp it
But I still don't accept it

What does it mean?
What should I believe?
What should I think?

Where should I go?
Where should I strive?
Where should run?

It all seems so useless
It all seems so senseless
It all seems so empty

Here I am, once more
Here I am writing, once more
Here I am praying, once more

I want to strive
I want to believe
I want to succeed

I want to care
I want to love
I want to cherish

All these feelings
All these emotions
All this passion

cannot be in vain.

Lord, why did you give me all this?
Lord, why did you put me here?
Lord, why did you made me see him?

Faith, is about trust
Faith, is about love
Faith, is about hope

I want to hope
I want to believe
I want to dream

that there's hope
that there's some truth

that theres's so much more

My God,
What am I supposed to do?

My God,
What am I supposed to hope?

My God,
What am I supposed to do?

Should I fight?
Should I scream?
Should I run away?

I'm so tired
I'm so broken
I'm so lost

I have no idea

what's going on
what will happen
what he thinks

Dear Lord,
give me clarity

Dear Lord,
give me hope

Dear Lord,
give me strength

Glorious perseverance
Beautiful patience
Timeless Serenity

I know what I want
I know what I long for
I know what I hope for

But I don't know if it's right
But I don't know if it's Your will
But I don't know if he wants it too

Maybe It's all in my head
Maybe I'm all alone
Maybe I'm the only one who cares

Does it matter?

Your are my Destination
Lord

Your are my True Love
Lord

You are my All
Lord

Protect me
Cherish me
Guide me

I am so lost

I did it for You
I give it all to You
I followed Your voice

Was I wrong?
Was I right?
Was I blinded?

Maybe it was all me
Maybe it was only my heart
Maybe it was only a daydream

But I really thought
I was doing it for You

But I really thought
I was serving You

But I really thought
I was listening to You

And then,
I got lost

And then,
I lost my way

And then,
I forgot my purpose

Dearest Lord
Dearest Love
Dearest Light

You are All that matters
You are All that is true
You are All that I care for

Free me from this maze

Free me from this lie
Free me from this nightmare

It was a dream
It was a vision
It was a story

but it became a nightmare.

Oh I still wish for it
Oh I still hope for it
Oh I still long for it

but if it's not Your Will
but if it's not Your desire
but if it's not Your wish

then open my eyes
then let me go
then set me free

Free from destructive passion
Free from selfish love
Free from my dream

Take me to Your Light
Take me to Your Peace
Take me Home

I cannot go on like this
I cannot go on breaking down
I cannot go on crying

I don't want to compare myself to others
I don't want to desire what others have

I don't want to desire what I cannot have

Set me free
Set me free
Set me free

But I can't leave
But I can't give up
But I can't let go

Dear God,
there's so much I have to say to him

Dear God,
there's so much I have to know from him

Dear God,
there's so much love I want to give him

Maybe I'm wrong
Maybe You're protecting me
Maybe he's just a dream

I should walk away
I should run away
I should hid away

I should come back to Your arms
I should stay in Your arms
I should wait in Your arms

until the time is right
until You have found him
until You have decreed

But Dear Love,

I want it so much

But Dear Love,
I love so much

But Dear Love,
I hope so much

The road was so grey
The road was so lonely
The road was so cold

And then I saw hope
And then I saw a glimmer
And then I saw a lush green tree

It brought me close to you
It brought me close to the sun
It brought me close to myself

But I don't know anymore
But I don't see anymore
But I don't hear anymore

I dreamt so hard
I hoped so much
I believed too much

And here I am

The road seems even more grey
The road seems even more lonely
The road seems even more cold

so cold
like my soul

so cold
like my heart

so cold
like my anger

Yes, I am angry
Yes, I am sad
Yes, I am furious

Forgive me.
Heal me.
Help me.

Stupid man
Idiotic boy
Ridiculous child

Don't you see?
Don't you hear?
Don't you understand?

All that I can give you
All that I can share with you
All that I can love you

Maybe you do
Maybe you don't
Maybe you don't have any idea

How loud I'm screaming
How high I'm jumping
How far I'm reaching

it's my greatest gift

it's my truest gift
It's my deepest gift

So precious
So true
So genuine

So many years
So many chances
So many faces

But I've kept it all
But I've saved it all
But I've hid it all

Until I saw you
Until I heard you
Until I felt you

And now,
I would give it all to you

And now,
I would bestow it all to you

And now,
I would share it all with you

Without regret
Without a doubt
Without fear

I was supposed to be a boy
I was supposed to be a bad boy

But instead

I'm a girl
I'm a good girl

I want to throw it all away
I want to push it all away
I want to destroy it all

And holler
And scream
And roar

like a wild thing
like a survivor
like a free spirit

But I'm good
But I'm strong
But I'm in control

for You
for My Lord
for My Creator

Let it all go
Let it all melt
Let it all fade

Open my heart
Open my soul
Open my senses

Let light descend into me
Let truth descend into me
Let freedom descend into me

I am no beggar
I am no alley cat
I am no savage

I am a lady
I am a queen
I am Yours

I will not break down
I will not run away
I will not burn away

I will keep my eyes on You
I will keep my heart with You
I will keep my face towards You

Dancing with the music
Dancing in the night
Dancing with myself

then the blessed silence
then the gentle stillness
then the loving peace

I know now
that I will survive

I know now
that it doesn't matter

I know now
that there's so much more

If it does happen
I will smile

If it doesn't happen
I will smile

As long as You are here
I will smile

Now
Forever
Eternity

There are so many mountains
There are so many hills
There are so many valleys

Theres's so much to do
There's so much to achieve
There's so much to dream

And time is fleet

What matters
is my light

What matters
is Your light

What matters
is my journey towards the Light

Love
Heartbreaks

Hopes
Reality

Dreams

Truth

From one coast
to the other

From one summit
to the other

From one cave
to the other

I will find my way
I will find my voice
I will find my way to You

As the night fades away
As the dawn nears
I am still

As the darkness is drifting away
As the light is glimmering
I am silent

As my heart is healing
As my soul is reaching out
I am at peace

I'm not anguished anymore
I'm not scared anymore
I'm not angry anymore

I heard Your voice
I heard Your people
I heard Your words

There is hope

There is a goal
There is a way

I will find it
I will follow it
I will master it

And find my way to you

Goodbye to the broken bridge
Goodbye to the dusty book
Goodbye to the closed door

There's a paved road next to it
There's a wonderful path next to it
There's a magical highway next to it

My heart is not weeping anymore
My soul is not yearning anymore
My dreams are not broken anymore

My whole being is filled by

Your light
Your love
Your strength

I have been saved
I have been healed
I have been lifted

There's so much I can give
There's so much I will give
There's so much I'm giving

To the world

To humanity
To You

My hands are Yours
My mind is Yours
My work is Yours

I choose the light
I choose hope
I choose love

I choose trust
I choose faith
I choose patience

I choose beauty
I choose silence
I choose courage

I know now
that it will be fine

I know now
that I will find my way

I know now
that I will still love

Whatever happens
whatever I loose

Whatever happens
whatever I let go

Whatever happens
whatever I leave

I will go on
towards You

I will go on
towards my destiny

I will go on
towards the light

There's a purpose
There's a hope
There's a way

Thank you
to all those people sharing their hope

Thank you
to all those loved ones encouraging me

Thank you
to You my Creator.

From anger to peace
From anguish to love
From loss to thankfulness

Love
forever

Hope
forever

Faith

forever

50

Dearest Lord

Dearest Lord
Dearest Creator
Dearest All

I prayed every night
I cried every night
I begged every night

And you gave me a miracle
And you gave me hope
And you gave me a gift

Grateful tear
Grateful relief
Grateful respite

And now I'm trembling
And now I'm scared
And now I'm terrified

Is it real?
Is it possible?
Is it true?

They all think I'm brave
They all think I'm fearless
They all think I'm bold

But I'm so scared

Only to You can I whisper this
Only to You can I confide
Only to You can I ask :

Make me brave
Make me strong
Make me tough

There is a door
There is a path
There is a stream

I am so afraid

I wanted it so bad
I fought for it so bad
I dreamt of it so bad

and here it is…

Now I remember

Dear God,

I'm beaten down
once more

I'm on my knees
once more

I'm so tired
once more

Help me.

Open my eyes
Open my soul
Open my heart

Fill me up
Raise me up

Fill me with your light
Fill me with your grocer
Fill me with your strength

Change my face
Change my fate
Give me faith

I'm desperate
I'm empty

I'm useless

But I know,
that one day

But I hope,
that one day

But I pray,
that one day

This darkness will be filled with light
This loneliness will be filled with laughter
This emptiness will be filled with fire

I'm not scared

I know that it will change
I know that there's hope
I know that I'm not alone

I never was alone
I never will be alone
I never could be alone

Since I have You
Since I have my God
Since I have my Love

I am saved
I am healed
I am strong

With Your Light
With Your Hand
With Your Grace

I am safe
I am strong
I am still here

Let them hurt me
Let them hurl me
Let them hurdle me

They will not break me
They will not drown me
They will not stop me

My life is Yours
My heart is Yours
My soul is Yours

The world may crash and burn
The towers may crash and burn
My heart may crash and burn

I am free
I am Yours
I am free

Forgive me for forgetting my purpose
Forgive me for forgetting you
Forgive me for forgetting myself

Why did I except from him
Only what You can give?

Why did I seek in him
Only what You can give?

Why did I beg him for

Only what You can give?

Forgive me,
My only True Love

Hold me,
My only True Love

Protect me,
My only True Love.

Take all my tears
Take all my fears
Take all my all

Why did I think I didn't need You?
Why did I betray you?
Why did I run away?

Why did I get blinded ?
Why did I get deafened ?
Why did I get broken?

I belong only to You
I desire only You
I run only to You

Let me in
Let me let go
Let me in

From Your arms I came
To Your arms I will return

From Your light I came
To Your light I will return

From your breath I came
To Your breath I will return

I misunderstood my purpose
I forgot my purpose
I lost my purpose

But now I remember
But now I hear
But now I know

that my only purpose is

to love You
to serve You
to give You

All my heart
All my soul
All of my life

Forever.

Forgive me
Protect me
Love me.

I thought I lost everything
I thought I failed everything
I thought I had nothing left

But I was wrong
But I was blind
But I was a fool

I have found everything
I have achieved everything
I have everything

I have Your love
I have Your light
I have You

Don't let me forget
Don't let me get lost
Don't let me fall

Your Peace
Your Love
Your Strength

Flows into my broken heart
Flows into my fading soul
Flows into me.

I was so hurt
I felt so humiliated
I felt so lost

But I was wrong…

There was always light
There was always love
There was always You

Forgive me.

Gentle prayer

May I be a shining light
May I have a shining heart
May I have a shining soul

White and Clear
Silver and Glittering
Transparent and Soft

As pure as a mountain brooke

Graceful
Kind
Loving

A pure vessel of Love
A pure vessel of Compassion
A pure vessel of Light

Giving
Receiving
Loving

Loving you for God

We are both side by side in this torrent of love
But our eyes are not gazing at each other
we long for the light beyond

Willingly we'd die for Him
Side by Side

Willingly we'd sacrifice all for Him
Side by Side

Willingly we'd give our all to Him
Side by Side

What we share
is tenderness

All the emotion
All the yearning
All the desire

is for Him.

And side by side
We serve him

And side by side
We praise Him

And side by side
We call to Him

We are merely

Companions
Friends
Siblings

Our love
Our soul
Our selves

are for Him.

And side by side
we will live
And side by side
we will give
And side by side
we will die.

Hand in Hand
we will face death

Hand in Hand
we will face judgement

Hand in Hand
We will melt into Him.

Even if you die
Even if I die
He will be here for us

Even if you leave
Even if I leave
He will always be here

Even if you betray me
Even if I betray you
He will be here for us,

He is our Father
He is our Mother
He is our Home

The Destination
The Light
The Truth

And it is for him that I long
And it is for him that I cry
And it is for him that I struggle

They may call me a fool
They may call me a dreamer
They may call me zealot

They keep on talking about love…

Isn't this love?

There's only One

There is only one Refuge
There is only one Peace
There is only one Salve

There is only one River
to quench my thirst.

There is only one Sun
to warm my cold skin.

There is only one Earth
to treasure each step I make.

There is only Thee My God.
There is only Thee My God.
There is only Thee My God.

Thou art from whence I came.
Thou art where I will return.
Thou art the Keeper of my soul.

Stand together

The darkness grows

from mankind to mankind
from the earth to the stars
from the oceans to the land

Doubt
Anger
Distrust

Between brothers and sisters
Between husband and wives
Between friends and companions

Those whispers
reach from the depth of darkness

Those whispers
strangle from the depth of darkness

Those whispers
drown from the depth of darkness

Kinship
Sisterhood
Brotherhood

Stand arm to arm
Stand shoulder to shoulder
Stand side by side

Open your heart
Open your hands
Open your eyes

And listen
And embrace
And forgive.

We are one people
We are one family
We are one.

They brew
poisonous draughts

They print
poisonous stories

They weave
poisonous webs

But you have a soul
But you have a heart
But you have a mind

Listen, don't merely hear
Welcome, don't merely tolerate
Help, don't only merely give

Give with your heart
Give with your time
Give with your treasures.

Stand,
Hand in hand

Arm in arm
Soul to soul.

For their clever lies
For their bitter strife
For their sly efforts

are nothing but dust
are nothing but ashes
are nothing but noise

Our hearts shine the brighter
Our souls soar the higher
Our love grows the loftier

When we stand together
When we strive together
When we soar together

One sisterhood
One brotherhood
One kinship

One universe
One humanity
One civilization

One love
One loyalty
One Ummah,

Filled with kindness
Filled with gentleness
Filled with forgiveness

For all

For all humans
For all creatures

And an abundance of love
And an eternity of love
And an infinity of love

For the Creator
For the Lover
For the Protector.

Loving those in the Ummah
Loving those out of the Ummah
Loving because of the Ummah.

That link
That kinship
That shelter

From the darkness
From the mischief
From the evil

Of those who poison
Of those who manipulate
Of those who mislead

My brother
My sister
My child

My parent
My grandparent
My great grand parent

Stranger in the street

Stranger in the web
Stranger in the maze

You are mine.

Let me give you,
my love.

Let me give you,
my strength.

Let me give you,
my embrace.

Let me share
Let me give
Let me bestow

The gifts given to me.

An overflowing fountain of love
An abundant ocean of love
An infinite supernova of love

For all,
For my ummah,
For my kin.

Only a man

Dearest Love
Dearest Creator
Dearest God

Forgive me
Embrace me
Love me

I was wrong
I was blinded
I was misguided

How could I think he could replace you?
How could I think he meant more than you?
How could I think he was all I needed?

You are the keeper of my soul
You are the keeper of my heart
You are the keeper of my life

Oh Lord

he's only a man
he's only a dream
he's only a human

and you are my all
and you are my everything
and you are my eternity

Can't ask him

for what only you can give me
for what only you can show me
for what only you can tell me

Forgive me

Make me forget him
Make me go on
Make me accept him

And let me in
And let me breathe
And let me be loved by you

What is missing
is you

What is burning me
is you

What I'm longing for
is you

My pain
My fear
My doubts

erase them

I thought
I believed
I tried

but I was wrong

Show me how to let it all go
Show me how to accept it
Show me how to keep on going

Don't let met forget

the destination
True love
the goal

All I need
is Your love

All I need
is Your embrace

All I need
is Your absolution

I feel so disconnected
I feel so far away
I feel so numbed

Open my heart
Open my eyes
Open my soul

and remind me
and fill me with light
and guide me

Mystical Wildness

Naked
Vulnerable
Melting

Bare skin against the mud
Frozen toes dipping into velvet
Dry lips guzzling down water

Butterfly wings
Violet petals
Flutter of wings

Closer and closer
Further and further

The warmth of the sun seeping into each pore

Luscious
Vibrante
So thick

Trees
Pines
Needles

So flagrant!

And then blew the wind

Furious

Indomptable
Destructive

Leaving me here

Rolling in the mud
Clawing in the dirt
Crying in the darkness

Where is the moon?
Where are the trees?
Where is life?

Will I bleed if I push the blade in?
Or will soot trickle out?
Or will a sigh rush out?
Or will bitter bile claw out?

Will I finally breathe and stand up?

Waiting for the leaves to fall
Waiting for the mist to rise
Waiting for the wind to come again

And take me

Beyond this valley
Beyond this state
Beyond this body…

Ah to glide

Through Time
Through Space
Through Existence

Forgetting the gift of a flower
Forgetting the gift of a fondant
Forgetting the gift of a fantasy

Melting into Being
Melting into Consciousness
Melting into Eternity

away from my mortal limbs

I need to go home

The soul yearns,

Whispering
Lamenting
Weeping,

Let me go home.

A pain that no heart can know
A need that no body can know
A cry that no mind can know

It's a flutter in the stillness
It's a hush in the howling
It's a rustling in the bush

I want to go home

The hearts beats calling itself a home
The body carves and craves a home
The mind creates and names a home…

What are feelings
What are walls
What are doors

To a soul ?

Entrapped into a room
Entrapped into a life

Entrapped into a body

A slowly decaying body
A weakly responding body
A creaky struggling body

I long for my home, sighs the soul

The heart listen and weeps
The body listens and sleeps
The mind listens and creates

Echoing the cry of so many

I need to go home.

Together for the primordial promise

I stood in the dark
I stood in the light
I stood in the cold

They twinkle so far away
They dwindle so far away
They kindle so far away

My feet anchored on the cold stone

Not a sigh
Not a fly
Not a sky

A dark miasma
A cold chiasma
An elusive enigma

Alone so very alone
Alive so very alive
Empty so very empty

Atoms and elements
Spirit and might
Soul and heart

Like tendrils
Like vine

Like lace

Clinging
Swinging
Stinging

Poison Ivy
Belladonna
Apple core

Oh the universe was but beginning
Oh the universe was but ending
Oh the universe was but existing

And I was the light
And I was the darkness
And I was the black matter

I was a sentinel
I was a sentiment
I was a sediment

That brought life
That connected life
That ate life

Like you
Like them
Like us

History far beyond history

Through galaxies
Through veils
Through eternities

The silent voyage of the souls

We were more than flesh and being
We were more than bones and nails
We were more than teeth and tears

Ever expanding light
Ever expanding darkness
Ever expanding cosmos

From us to us
From the past to the future
From the now to the then

We are still there

Watching
Gnawing
Waiting

For the envol
For the return
For the moment

Before time
After time
In time

Ah dearest,

You lost your way
You lost your mind
You lost your soul

And you cannot remember

Taste the ashes of the stars
Hear the moans of the planets
Feel the caress of the dark matter

And you cannot remember

The first Home
The first Kiss
The first Breath

Ah dearest!

I was sent to heed you
I was sent to hear you
I was sent to heal you

Remember as we flew
Remember as we grew
Remember as we view

How the story would unfold
How our hearts would hold
How our souls were mold

Ah dearest,
Hear the silence of the stars
Ah dearest,
smell the flagrance of the rocks
Ah dearest,
feel the expansion of matter

Can you remember?

For we stood in the dark
For we stood in the light
For we stood in the cold

Hand in hand
Heart to heart
Soul to soul

Unafraid of the great unfold
Unafraid of the great untold
Unafraid to behold

What dangers the universe offered.
What quest Our Lord offered
What pain our hearts offered.

Alone we shall float forever
Alone we shall burn forever
Alone we shall collapse forever

But together,

We can climb
We can grasp
We can catch

The last Light
the last Hope
the last Return

Ah dearest,
let me hold you and sing of that time.

The forgotten princess

Nightingales are chirping
The full moon is rising
My mind is crashing

It has been too long
It has been too far
I am tired.

I roll to bed
I twist under my sheet
I turn to the wall

My limbs are heavy
my feet stiff and weary
My neck barely steady

I did fight the good fight

Years and years
Seasons and seasons
Centuries and centuries

My skin is turning into paper
My lips are turning into pebbles
My stomach is turning into mush

Nothing is left but a spark

Oh you see it from afar

That far off star
That far off dream
That far of chimera

Once bestowed upon you

The treasure is buried
The box is empty
Tthe emptiness is bitting

Cruel even,
oh so bitter.

The oracle raises her heavy arms
The priestess ground her weary feet
The seeress straighten her barely steady neck

She peers into the web of stars
She peers into the waves of dark matter
She peers into the craggy full moon

Her hand on her belly
the other one reaching up

Asking her Deity
Her eyes raising up

Asking for clarity
Her feet lifting her up

And sees,
galaxies and spiderwebs

And hears,
nightingales and sparrows

And touch
the ground and the beyond

All within reach,
in one breath.

Eye after eye
Palm after palm
Heartbeat after heartbeat

She opens up.

Where there is a spark, there is enough to light a
night.
Where there is a spark, there is enough to warm a
winter.
Where there is a spark, there is enough to build a
home.

I let out a breath
I sigh
and I cry

Deep in slumber

The dawn birds start to chirp
The sun starts to peak through the curtains
And I stretch my toes

And I know.
Oh, how I know!

And I am free.
Oh, how I am free!

And I love!

Oh, how I love.

My doubts have been dusted away
My fears have been raked away
My tears have been wiped away

You may be a mockingbird
You may be a passing cloud
You may be a fading chimera

But I am here

Solid legs
Strong stomach
and straight shoulders

I breathe and I drink
I breathe and I eat
I breathe and I walk.

In the arms of my Creator, I am beyond needs.

You may flit by
You may flicker by
You may fly by

In His Presence I am safe.

You may hold me for years
You may kiss me for years
You may sway me for years

In His Light I am light.

No fear.

Free to run through the woods

I was born for the woods
I was born for the marshes
I was born for the mountains…

In a world of

Amnesia
Ammonia
Anesthesia.

From running to tiptoeing
From climbing to falling
From hollering to whimpering

Wild wind scaring me
Ominous owls scaring me
Shadowy shapes scaring me

Because I had forgotten,

My true nature
My true call
My true home.

Fairy of the mud
Creature of the vale
Soul of the galaxy

Daughter of healers
Daughter of leaders
Daughter of mystics

Belonging to the night
Belonging to the moon
Belonging to the silence

Far far from this race
Far far from this game
Far far from this delusion

Living in the Light of Truth
Living in the Light of Eternity
Living in the Light of Love

Seeking
Soaring
Sending

So much love and joy.

But the steel bit into my skin.
But the asphalt burnt my skin.
But the fumes choked my skin.

And I forgot.

I wandered from sadness to excitement,
I ran from pleasure to disgust
I crashed from despair to more despair

Feeling this void
Feeling this pain
Feeling this thirst

Tumbling down into a frozen hell.

Helpers,
Healers,
Teachers,

You sent me.

And I heard in their voices
And I felt in their embraces
And I smelled in their breath

Your Call
Your Love
Your Being

And I was free

To run through the woods
To patter through the marshes
To stride to the mountains.

And climb to higher peaks
And climb to higher states
And climb to higher pastures.

I was free.

In His presence

The wind is roaring
The rain is pounding
The cold is burning

These walls have been empty for too long

They haven't felt your gaze on their wood
They haven't felt your weight on their planks
They haven't heard your voice on their panes

They no longer remember your presence

And yet,

As I stretch my hands to the sky
As I whirl my body to the sky
As I reach my soul to the sky

My love for you spreads like a web over the earth

Gathering stars in its net
Weaving planets in its filament
Beading sunbeams in its core

Spreading like light

From East to West
From South to North
From Distance to Time

Can you hear my song?
Can you feel my arms?
Can you feel my gaze?

Lulling you to safety
Wrapping you home
Capturing you into light

I listen to the wind roaring
I watch the rain pounding
I feel the cold curling

To see a sign
To hear a message
To feel a presence

How can you be close, yet so far?

A glimpse away
A breath away
A dream away

Maybe in slumber, I can hear your voice
Maybe in stillness, I can feel your presence
Maybe in sunlight, I can see your eyes

My mind is an ever expanding universe
My mind is an ever collapsing universe
Far and Near

All and One

In His presence we are face to face,
In His presence we are hand in hand,
In His presence, we are soul to soul,

Two pieces of the same veil

Flapping in the wind
Shredding in the rain
Freezing in the cold

What use is a patch of fabric?

Unwanted
Discarded

Fly, fly to me

Whisper after whisper
Moans after moans
whimper after whimper

Into a lullaby
Into a serenade
Into a hymn

Hum it to the strangers
Belt it out to the world
Psalm it to the silence

Perchance, God may hear it
And collapse the distance
And melt the time

And fill this empty dungeon of mine.

In Eternity's soft silence

As my heart thud painfully against my chest
As my breath itches in my dry throat
As the world around me spins without control

I close my eyes and rise.

Rise above the roof
Rise above the clouds
Rise above the sky

Into the pure darkness
Into the pure stillness
Into the pure nothingness

Space
Eternity
Time stops

The universe unfolds in front of my eyes

Galaxies die and are born
Stars collapse and sparkle
Planets expand into infinity

I am but a speck
I am but a whisper
I am but a moment

In Eternity's infinity
In Eternity's velvet darkness

In Eternity's soft silence

As the universe expands and collapses

I am nothing
I am calm
I am at peace

Truth remains

Truth belongs to the patient
Truth belong to the resilient
Truth belong to the constant

Deeply buried under the earth
Deeply buried under the ice
Deeply buried under the ashes

Truth waits…

To that hunter that waited forever under the ice.
for justice

To that princess that waited forever under the sand
for love.

To those lovers that waited forever under the earth
for absolution.

Lost
Forgotten
Found.

Yet a mystery until the last day…

For what do we know of the time
when these valleys were embracing glaciers?

For what do we know of the time
when humanity was a speck in a never-ending

tundra?

For what do we know of the time
when those now forgotten lands sung with triumph?

Pieces
Dust
Embers.

And so many theories held as truth
And so many history books held as truth
And so many mythical legends held as truth.

Until the turn of the tide.

A new storyteller
A new weaver
A new jester

Creates an empire of gold and ashes.

Have you travelled through those roads?
Have you travelled through those passes?
Have you travelled through those bridges?

And felt…

Soft tendril
Distant flickers
Muted echoes

The past is forgotten
The past is fragmented
The past is ever returning.

Like the waxing and waning of the pearl

Like the rise and fall of the golden phoenix
Like the surge of light and death within a maiden.

Pulsating
Vibrant
Warm

Life.

What lives,
never dies.

What dies,
always returns.

What lives and dies,
tells the truth.

Did you see?
Did you hear?
Did you understand?

Patience,
Let your heart beat.

Patience,
Let your mind breathe.

Patience,
Let your soul beam.

Soar,
Glide,
Rise…

Do you see it now?

The season of the continents,
Ever shifting.

The season of the planets,
Ever transforming.

The season of the atoms,
Ever remembering.

Like a dance,

Twirl
Turn
and whirl.

Words are never erased,
from a paper.

Hovels are never raised
to the ground.

Hopes are never cast,
to the seas -

Without returning.

A chimera.
A ghoul,
A ghost…

A reminder.
A secret.
A spell.

Written within the bark of a tree.

Whispered in an ice core
Weaved in thick amber.

For those who see
For those who seek.
For those who feel…

The echoes of your last breath.
The reverberation of your precious life.
The melody of the Truth within you.

Centuries ago,
Millenniums ago,
Ages and ages ago,

And now buried in time.

Until the land rocks and slides.
Until the ice breaks and melts.
Under the seas recede and boil over.

Truth remains,
Until the end of the times.

On the same path

After the rushing trickles,
After the hurried gasps,
After the crackling fires,

There's a pool.

Calm,
Motionless,
Reflecting

The blaze of the sun.
The gleam of the moon.
The glimmer of the stars.

Reflecting deeply.

No sorrow
No joy
No sigh.

What is gone, is gone.
What is left, is left.
What is, is.

… But what is that?

Tell me, please, tell me.
Write again, please, write again.
Hope once more, please, hope once more.

But the boulders have rolled down.
But the wind has died down.
But the birds have settled down.

And there are no answers.

The river is black with ink.
The river is gray with tears.
The river is white with remembrance.

Until I saw the crescent moon.

I left the cabin in the woods.
I left the room full of books.
I left the two cups of tea.

And I kept on walking.

Stone in my chest.
Ashes in my throat.
Brambles in my eyes.

And I kept on walking.

Tears tickling down,
Hope dashing away,
Dreams buried away,

And I kept on walking.

Parched lips.
Rumbling stomach.
Empty heart.

Found, found my way.
Away, away to find.

Found my way back home.

To What is beyond those stars.
To What is higher than this sun.
To What is more real than reality.

Home.

Tell me love,
Weren't you headed this way too?

Tell me my sparrow,
Weren't we headed this way together?

Tell me my oak tree,
Were we longing for the same destination?

As I walk on,

I can see your eyes,
I can hear your words,
I can feel your warmth,

In a flash,
In a flutter,
In a twinkle,

Of my heart.

Maybe, as I make my way Home,
Maybe, as I make my way to Freedom.
Maybe, as I make my way to Peace.

Around the bend I will find,

A kindred spirit,

A fellow wanderer.
A familiar presence.

Fingers entwined,
Palm to palm,
Souls entwined,

We will walk side by side, again.

Never parting,
Never cleaving,
Never untangling

Until we reach Our Destination.

Return to the Source

When waves of human love confuse me
When winds of human rage ensnare me
When fumes of human desire bewitch me

I can no longer breathe deeply.
I can no longer hear deeply.
I can no longer love deeply.

And I wonder,
And I wander,
And I wound her.

The soul within me,
The heart within me,
The light within me

Are wounded
Are dulled
Are rusted.

Wounded.
Blinded.
Confused.

There's a stir within me
There's a spark within me
There's a call within me.

That can never be lost.

As I feel the warm ground beneath my feet.
As I hear the gentle chirp of the sparrows above my

head.
As I smell the teardrop in the air around my body.

I find that pathway….

Through the woods,
Through the clearing,
To the cabin

Where the fire never dies.

Yesterday I shivered.
Yesterday I heaved.
Yesterday I whispered.

What will happen to me

Once, this gentle love is soothed.
Once this gentle touch has vanished.
Once this gentle grasp has faded.

Will I return to myself?
Will I return home?
Will I return to You?

For returning I must…

I cannot sense You.
I cannot hear You.
I cannot hold You,

I cannot be regenerated by Your Light.

How afraid I was yesterday…

Yet today,

The waves,
The winds,
The fumes

all faded.

The sparrows are pecking.
The doves are cooing,
The woodpeckers are seeking,

What I already have.
What I never lost.
What I always keep…

Your Presence.

It was only my heart that was too loud.
It was only my mind that was too loud.
It was only the world that was too loud.

It all recedes

When I seek for You.
When I call for You.
When I reach for You.

From all my being.

Body
Heart
Soul.

All for my all.
My all for All.
All.

You are The Source of all Love.

You are The Source of all Light.
You are the Source of all Life.

They may come,
They may leave.

They may love,
They may hate.

They may try,
They may give up.

But you were the First.
But you are the Constant.
But you will be the Last.

Destination,
Refuge,
Home.

The sparrows,
The raindrops
And even the airplanes

Sing your praise.

The tired soil
The weakened trees
The faltering roses

All long for Your Mercy,

That You pour on us,

Drop after drop,
Wave after wave,

Cloud after cloud.

Glimmer of a lost star

Did you wake up at midnight?
Did you open your window tonight?
Did you look up to the night?

They would say,

Why bother?
Why care?
Why try?

It's raining too much.
It's too cold.
It's too cloudy.

But you wouldn't…

Because you dream.
Because you hope.
Because you believe.

So you woke up.

Barefoot,
Barhead,
Barehanded,

You went to meet the night.

No moon glimmering.
No stars glinting.

No eyes glinting.

Only the darkness,
Only the silence,
Only Your Creator,

A breath in,
Heart beating,
A breath out,
Heart beating.
A breath in.

And you see it…

As if your eyes could pierce
The clouds

As if your eyes could travel beyond,
The atmosphere.

As if your eyes could see
The unseen.

There's a star.

Behind the thick clouds,
Behind the ashen sky,
Behind the shivering twilight,

There's a star

Beckoning you.
Calling you.
Lulling you..

Brave,

Steadfast,
Earnest.

You've seen it before,
Haven't you?

You've heared it before,
Haven't you?

You've sang it before,
Haven't you?

That hymn to Hope.
That praise to the Light
That prayer to God

With that same star.

Remember, that twinkle,
Do remember.

Remember, that whisper,
Do remember.

Remember that promise,
Do remember.

In that time before time.
In that space before space.
In that moment before moment.

When you faced Your Creator.

And you knew,
what you know now.

And you believed,
What you believe now.

And you saw,
What you see now…

In the glimmer of a lost star.

Shelter from history

I seek a cocoon
I seek a warm bed
I seek safety

Heart in my throat
Earring in the drain
Rage in the web

Too silent
Too loud
Thudding heart.

Too loud
Too silent
Thudding march

Too loud
Too silent
Thudding bullets

They fear the clown
They fear the image
They fear the puppet

I fear chaos
I fear unrest
I fear reaction

Neighbors
and mass graves

Legislator
and mass deportations

Friends
and mass denunciation

Unseeing
Unfeeling
Unthinking

They throw stones at the puppet

He laughed
He rejoiced
He burns

It doesn't matter

What is asked is chaos
What is planned is civil war
What is oncoming is the storm

A storm
blasting trough friendships

A storm
sweeping through amendments

A storm
carving through civilization

They fear the puppet
I fear them

They condemn the puppet

I condemn them

They accuse the puppet
I accuse them

Their voices are raised
Their fists are raised
Their guns are raised

Blasting
Burning
Brutalizing

As evil as a man may be
he is no mob

As evil as a man may be
he is no herd

As evil as a man may be
he is no army

It is the crowd
we must warn

It is people
we must calm

It is you and me
we must reason

From a spark is spread a wildfire

Burning
Cascading
Molting

the whole world.

I can feel the waves
I can feel the gusts
I feel the whispers

It is coming.

I can feel the rage
I can feel the blindness
I can feel the violence

Seeping from my screen
Spreading from my phone
Swimming into my home

trying to contaminate us
trying to control us
Trying to coerce us

to become the persecutor
to become the tormentor
to become the executioner

of your own brother
of your own child
of your own father

For words excavated on the mountain
For words bled on the pages
For words screaming on the screen

For words never understood
For words always understood.

They wait,
the shadows

They wait,
the whisperers

They wait,
the never bleeding

For one call
For one cry
For one shot

And they will swarm
And they will scatter
And they will camper

In our thoughts
In our halls
On our shoulders

Guiding our hands
Guiding our lips
Guiding our step

To the point of no return
To the brink of the storm
To the edge of the ocean

Oily black water
unmerciful shredding waves
Unknowable abysses

Many of us starve
Many of us wait
Many of us desire

this wave
this push
this attraction

To the edge of a knife
To the bottom of a grave
To the mindless frenzy.

Some will stand
Some will pray
Some will love

Hoping,
that words save the world

Hoping,
that prayer change their hearts

Hoping,
that love melt their armor

But the trigger has been pulled
But the song has begun
But the macabre dance is open

Come and dance with them

Bloodied feet
Stained cheeks
Parched lips

And no eyes
never see.

And no teeth

never speak.

And no arms
never embrace.

All of them sanctimonious
All of them self righteous
All of them ceremonious

They believe
They know
They never doubt

That their hands are pure
That their war is pure
That their conscience is pure.

Dancing
killing

Singing
throttling

Bowing
burying.

Chanting,
that they are right.

Chanting
that they are blameless

Chanting
that they are the good ones.

Where is their bed?

Where is their home?
Where is their safe place?

Under a puddle
Under a grave
Under a lie

Frenzy
Fury
Ferocity

Mad cattle
Wild herd
Unchaperoned madmen

Who will stop them?

I can hear their hiss
I can hear their pants
I can hear their steps

I lock my door
I lock my heart
I lock my soul

And hope

I will not lose my head
I will not lose my heart
I will not lose my love.

It is coming,
the great wave,

It is coming
the great mass,

It is coming,
the great finale.

And I seek for a shelter
And I seek for a home
And I seek for a burrow

I hear Your voice
I hear the silence

I have become deaf
Have I become deaf?

I have become blind
Have I become blind?

I have become mad
Have I become mad?

Or is it here,
right at the edge

Or is it here,
right at the end

Or is it here,
right at the corner

that I will finally wake up
That I will finally see again
That I will finally breathe again

And be safe,

In Your arms

In Your fortress
In Your love.

To the journey

Creature of the woods,
Creature of the wilds,
Creature of the winds…

Never of this city.

Blinding lights,
Deafening voices,
Intoxicating fumes.

I crawl back to my

Hovel
Cabin
Tower.

Nestled in the trees.

Aspens.
Oaks.
Maples.

Why must I leave my peace?
Why must I?

You must,
You shall,
You will, my child.

They call,

They always call…

Through the highways,
Through the valleys,
Through the seas,

They wake me up at night.

Child,
You must come.

Child,
You must run.

Child,
You must return.

And I look the other way.

Shivering,
Trembling,
Twitching,

There will be no rest,
Until I answer

This call
This beseech
This summon.

Too young,
Too soon,
Too fragile.

I cannot.

But my heart never rests.

And my face becomes finer.
And my eyes become deeper.
And my hair becomes lighter.

Time cannot ever be hindered.

Am I standing still, am I moving?

Dancing
Twirling
Balancing

Between two world.
Between two direction.
Between two paths.

How high is the tightrope!
How high is the horizon!
How high is the summit!

The river runs in the glen.
The daisies grow in the hollow.
The children play in the dale.

But I belong far away from

Their gushing.
Their dancing.
Their singing.

I wish I could climb down to them.
I wish I could run to them.
I wish I could stay with them.

Find smooth pebbles in the river.
Make luscious flower crowns,
Hold their small hands in mine.

I look at them.
I wave at them.
I call to them.

They never notice me.

There's an invisible veil between us.
Theres's an invisible net between us.
There's an invisible barrier between us.

Like the one that separates

Living from the dead,
Light from the shadows.
Freshwater from saltwater.

Invisible.
Subtle.
Unshakable.

Yet,
We must all flow.

Yet,
We must all fly.

Yet,
We must all feel….

The call beneath our ribs.
The call beneath our heart.
The call beneath our fingertips.

Can you hear it too?
Can you?

Or am I a madwoman…

Frenzied.
Frantic.
Free.

Ever wandering.
Ever solitary,
Ever thirsty,

Scattering behind me

Petals of what could have been,
Hums of what could perhaps be.
Feathers of what could never be.

Unless…

And I look away from the vale,
And I look to my own feet.
And I look up to the sky.

Unless…

Do you ever hear echoes of prayers,
Do you ever hear tatters of laments,
Do you ever hear hopeful hymns,

Up there in the lonely mountains?

Voices of those
Who journey.

Voices of those,
Who leave.

Voices of those,
Who must return.

To the Unknowable.
To the Unseeable.
To the Ungraspable.

To the ever Familiar.
To the ever Compassionate.
To the ever Loving.

And the voices…

Of those who sing in your blood.
Of those who whisper in your dreams.
Of those who are heard in your own words.

To a distant land.
To an ancient time.
To another idiom.

You can almost see it…

The scorching desert.
The freezing summits.
The haunting ruins.

Towers embroidered of

Gold
Turquoise
And blue.

You can feel them under your fingertips.
You can feel them against your palms.
You can feel them against your cheek.

Like a scent that never leaves you…

Musk
Frankincense
And roses.

And the chants,
And the oud
And the sitar.

Like a melody that lulls you

In,
Out,
and In,

Of a sleep carved with dreams.

A maddening labyrinthe

Curls,
Leaps
and fire out.

Burning,
Like a memory.

Burning,
Like a desire.

Burning,

Like a thirst.

Something you cannot have imagined.
Something you cannot translate in words.
Something you cannot explain with reason.

So you lie awake.

Wordlessly,
Hopelessly,
Mindlessly,

Listening.

Even in this peaceful forest,
Even in this gentle country lane,
Even in this blissful night,

Every breeze that breathes,
Every twig that creaks,
Every bird that leaps,

Echo those voices….

Calling you,
Beseeching you,
Summoning you,

To the journey.

Onwards

Deep rust dew,
Light golden sunbeam,
Soft pitter patter.

 Haven't I told you before?

I am not from this world.
I am not for this world.
I merely exist here.

The bridge I left behind

Fell apart as I stepped on it.
Dissolved as I stepped on it.
Blew away as I stepped on it.

I leaped over the abyss
I flew over the abyss
I rose over over the abyss.

The bridge in front of me

Is already wobbling.
Is already fading.
Is already whining.

I wish you were strong enough to catch me
I wish you were strong enough to hold me.
I wish you were strong enough to follow me.

Through the muddy path,
Over the sharp ridges,
Under the thick mossed earth.

Leaning over that void
Where you once stood.

Leaning over that well,
Where you once spoke.

Leaning over that crevasse
Where you once beckoned me.

I scatter pearls and feathers,
I scatter petals and ashes,
I scatter smoke and tears.

But I already know that it's in vain.

So I turn around,
I turn left,
and keep on turning left.

Until I find a whiff of

Myrrh
Frankincense
Roses.

and I find the stairwell,
and I find the base camp,
and I find the holy cave.

Where I can truly hear.
Where I can truly speak.
Where I can truly connect.

… And at last be understood.

Dear sparrow,

So gentle,
So constant,
So chatty.

I listen to you.
You listen to me.
Neither is understood.

I see you plunge into the fountain
Flap around your wings.

I see you plunge your beak,
Drink your fill.

How brave,
How endearing,
How beautiful.

But I am no bird…

What am I?

I look deep into that chasm,
I look deep into that smoke,
I look deep into that well,

And try to find an echo of me.

An apple tree,
An apple blossom,
An apple seed.

Nothing more.

A nurturing creature,
A loving heart,
And a promise to keep.

Find my shoots in spring,
Find my flowers in summer,
Find my fruits in autumn,
Find my bare core in the winter.

Ever glowing
Ever growing,
Ever giving.

But never yours.

I belong to the seasons,
I belong to the sunshine,
I belong to the rainfall.

I belong to the thick and rich soil.
I belong to the soft and warm sun.
I belong to the vigorous and living sap.

But foremost…

From my ever growing roots,
Through my solid core,
To my ever growing fruits,

I belong to

The One who created me.
The One who nourished me.

The One who protected me.

And to Whom I will return.

Listen to the bee,
Smell the winter jasmine,
Hold the fallen acorns.

It is not winter yet.
And yet, it will return.

How thin the veils between the worlds are.
How soft the voices calling to each other are.
How persistant the souls drawn to each other are.

Kismet.

Come, come closer…

Perhaps these woods are not haunted.
Perhaps that crone is not evil.
Perhaps that path isn't thorny.

Come, come closer…

Maybe I am wrong.
Maybe you are right.
Maybe…

 Come, come closer…

Perchance, this cabin isn't an illusion.
Perchance, this roaring fire isn't a dream.
Perchance, this embrace isn't a fantasy.

Destiny?

When the leaves fall,
One by one.

When the squirrels gather nuts,
One by one.

When the birds leave,
One by One.

I cannot see clearly.
The mists.

I cannot think clearly,
The bogs.

I cannot understand clearly,
The sunsets.

So short,
So short is a day.

So far,
So far we must go.

Will you follow me?

Home

You see

You were the spark
You were the scent
You were the silk

In my words.

From an acorn came a tale.
From a tale came a story.
From a story came an oak.

Under its shade,

I found peace.
I found solace
I found another spark,

Can you feel these deep roots?
Can you feel this thick bark?
Can you feel this rich foliage?

It is not you doing.
It is not your gift.
It is not yours.

Those are my words.
Those are my stories.
Those are my songs.

This is my oak tree.
Mine.

After you left,

It was my shelter
It was my home.
It was my ladder.

It led me to other stories
It led me to other discoveries.
It led me back home.

To my Creator.

You were but a breeze
You were but a gust of wind.
You were but a breath.

Long ago,
Long gone.
Gone.

Thank God.

Your roots didn't go deep enough.
Your arms were not strong enough.
Your heart was not wild enough.

To follow mine

Through the waves
Through the crags
Through the vales.

You didn't even try.

I must

Face the well.
Face the pond.
Face the mirror

And see what truly is here.

The stars,
The ebb,
Myself.

Alone.

Flesh, blood and alone.
Heart, lungs and alone.
Soul, dreams and alone.

Alone.

Not quite, not quite.

There's a thrill from that branch,
There's a flutter from within me,
There's a breath from far beyond.

I am never truly alone.

The finches on that branch,
The robin in my heart,
The bird of paradise in the horizon,

Simurgh

That calls me through the path

That calls me through the marshes
That call me through the mists

Back home.

Home, where is home?

To the endlessly wandering soul
To the utterly lost wild woman,
To the irresistibly inspired poet

Home is the Source and the Destination,
Home is the ever twisting clearway.
Home is the forest of inspiration.

That glowing window,
That warm alcove,
That gentle aroma.

You will never see it.
and I will never see you again.

Keep the golden blessings,
Keep the copper feelings,
Keep the silver yearnings.

Kindly
Peacefully
Absolutely.

As I retreat back

To my Refuge.
To my Source.
To my Light.

To return to the world,

With a brighter plumage,
With more colors in my feathers,
With a sweeter and deeper song.

In a wild and enchanted forest,
On a solid oak treel,
On a gentle twig,

Far far away from you.

Wordless

I may turn my head,
I may linger away,
I may crumble into dust.

When the sun rises through the curtain of trees,
When the sun dips behind the golden mountains,
When the sun glows from my own chest;

Glimmering gold dust caught in a beam,

I can feel You.
I can hear You.
I can heed You.

Like a warm embrace,
Like a soft wave,
Like an overwhelming elation.

No words can ever paint this.
No song can ever evoke this.
No painting can ever write this….

Look into my eyes,
Look into my words,
Look into my smile,

Do you see it now?

His Presence.
His Embrace.

His Mercy,

Faintly reflected in me.

Aren't we all a little bit

Opalescent,
Reverberating,
Echoing

That primordial Light,
That primordial Love,
That primordial Presence,

Our Creator?

I see it in you, dear friend.
Thank you.

When the illusions melt into the moss.
When the silence melts into a birdsong.
When the deception melts into the sunlight.

I can rise again.

And dance,
Step after step.

And walk,
Step after step.

And run,
Step after step.

And long for flight,

Like a bee,
Like a bird,
Like a prayer.

The muddy path cool under my barefoot
The thorny brambles spiky against my open palms.
The thick droplets so wet in my tangled hair.

Trickling,
Trickling
And sticking.

The rain is a blessing, my dear.
The rain is an offering, my dear.
The rain is a sign, my dear.

A sign of hope.
A sign of renewal,
A sign of rebirth.

Can you feel it?

Convulsing,
Trembling,
Quivering.

Oh so fresh and new!

Ideas spurting out like delicate mushrooms.
Ideas blooming out like fiery chrysanthemum
Ideas spreading like golden amber leaves.

You, oh You my Keeper, are whispering in the breeze.
You, oh You my Home, are sheltering me in the
woods.
You, oh You my Sustainer, are nurturing me with this

fire.

With every sputter,
With every flutter,
With every flicker,

Warmth spreads to my skin.
Warmth spreads to my limbs.
Warmth spreads to my heart.

Scampering away the dark ebbs.
Chasing away the whirling empty pool.
Flushing away the ashen specks

That taints my vision.
That sinks my spirit.
That cracks my will.

Let them roar.
Let them moan.
Let them croak.

My spirit remains untouched.

Safe,
Warm,
Encompassed

In Your Light.

Dear Love,
I call them love,
but You are My One True Love.

My Origin,
My Home,

My Destination.

The First,
The Ever-Present.
The Last

I do not wander in vain.
I do not seek in vain.
I do not linger in vain.

For my path takes me to,

Depths they cannot imagine,
Horizons they cannot comprehend,
Summits they cannot see.

Where even imagination isn't enough.
Where even introspection isn't enough.
Where even observation isn't enough.

Could I ever tell them about it?
Or will they also fly away?

Freedom,

They philosophy and lament about it.
They scatter off clothes and ties for it.
They follow every whim and fancy for it.

Freedom?
I ask.
Freedom?

Are you truly ready for it?

Mere mortals,

Mere animals,
Mere cells,

We are.

And yet,
And yet…

We stand at the edge

Of the ever expanding and contracting universes.
Of the ever spreading and shrinking atoms.
Of the ever departing and returning breath.

Within our selves,
Within our chest,
Within our souls.

Yes, my friend, do close your eyes .
Yes, my sister, do open your mouth.
Yes, my son, do listen with your ears.

And find the secrets nestled in your breath.
And find the gems scattered in your breath.
And find the peace nurtured in your breath.

Open your eyes,
and remember it always.

The secret,
The key,
The answer,

That we will never be able to explain.

No voice,

No claps,
No words;

Only the breath.